THE TRUTH ABOUT MORMONISM

Is It a Christian Church?

THE TRUTH ABOUT MORMONISM

Is It a Christian Church?

DR. HUGH PYLE

Post Office Box 1099 • Murfreesboro, Tennessee 37133

Printed and Bound in the United States of America

Dedication and Appreciation

I am most grateful to Dr. Wallace Higgins, Brother Al Price, and others of the Northwest Baptist Missions who have assisted me in this work with counsel, prayer and materials. Dr. Higgins, a graduate of Bob Jones University and Covenant Theological Seminary, is the founder and director of Northwest Baptist Missions and has done much to plant new churches in Mormon country. He has started or assisted in the start of some 25 churches in the West. Utah now has 29 independent Baptist churches of which 10 have been started by Northwest Baptist Missions, most in the last few years. Dr. Higgins has produced two radio broadcasts of the Gospel in Mormon territory. He does extensive speaking in missions conferences in churches across America and in Christian schools and colleges.

Pastor Harley Johnson was born and reared in Mormon country in the town of Craig, Colorado. When he graduated from high school, about half of his schoolmates went to Brigham Young University. Johnson went to Bob Jones University. He has helped me with many suggestions and updates on Mormon material and activities. He knows the Mormons well and serves as pastor of the Jordan Valley Baptist Church, West Jordan, Utah. He has helped me in rewriting Chapter 3 of this book and has given me valuable quotes on "the two sticks" and "baptism for the dead."

To these untiring servants of the Lord, the book, *The Truth About Mormonism,* is happily and prayerfully dedicated.

Hugh F. Pyle

Preface

What is this strange religion called Mormonism? Is it Christian? If not, what is it?

While conducting a youth revival in Mormon country (Idaho), I found the townspeople to be congenial. Yet there seemed to be a strange spirit about the place, so dominated by Mormons. Baptist mission workers had been given permission to rent the school for our services. Yet the Mormon custodian opened the door for us reluctantly, it seemed, and sometimes just barely in time for the service. Also he and other Mormons seemed always at hand to discourage the new converts. When one family came forward in the Baptist church the next Sunday and presented themselves for Christian baptism, it was with fear and trembling. They were already being persecuted for their new-found faith, and threats had been made if they continued on with the Lord.

I'm sure there are many fine, sincere Mormons. Many of these people have been raised Mormon, and they don't know anything else to believe. As I have read their literature and made a study of their teachings, my heart goes out to these dear ones who so need to hear the simple and glorious Gospel!

How does Mormonism differ from biblical Christianity?

Many of their teachings do not come from the Bible or from the *Book of Mormon!* A mother sobs (as many others have) to realize she cannot attend the wedding of her daughter in the Mormon temple. What goes on behind those closed doors that they do not want that mother *or* the rest of us to see? Why so secretive? Other churches gladly open their doors for visitors!

It all hinges on the tale of a young lad who in the early 1800s claimed he had found some gold plates buried in a New York hillside. He was a boy who loved fortunetelling and treasure seekers. He had a wild imagination, was somewhat gifted, and he read a lot. He was tried and convicted of being a glass looker (a crystal-gazing fortune-teller) in Bainbridge, N.Y., in 1826. It is said he only had eleven days of formal schooling, but many of the followers of Joseph Smith have accepted his religious ramblings as gospel truth.

Mormons claim that their membership now is well above 5 ½ million in 96 countries with 14,467 wards or congregations. They claim that every 2 minutes and 15 seconds someone joins the Mormon church and that the *Book of Mormon* has been translated into 67 languages.

Their church membership has increased by 29% during the past five years.

Joseph Smith, the founder of Mormonism, claimed that his church is a restoration of the true church that Christ established while on earth but which (they say) disappeared until Smith found the gold plates which an "angel of light" told him about in a vision in 1820. The Bible declares that Satan comes as "an angel of light" (II Cor. 11:14)! No one has really ever seen these gold plates which Smith says were written in "reformed Egyptian." He believed God commanded him to lead his followers to settle in "the land of Zion" (Missouri) in 1831.

Smith roamed from place to place and was accused of many misdeeds, including gross immorality and counterfeiting. He was arrested and jailed in Illinois. An angry mob stormed the prison, killing both Joseph Smith and his brother Hyrum.

Smith claimed to have translated the *Book of Mormon* from the gold plates under divine inspiration. Yet (to quote J. K. Van Baalen in *The Gist of the Cults*) the book contains such grammatical niceties as: "Yea, if my days had been in them days," and, "And they, having been waxed strong in battle, that they might not be destroyed," and, "Even until they had arriven at the land of Middoni"!

Mormonism teaches that "the miraculous conception is that Adam-God had sexual intercourse with Mary, with Jesus being the child" (Dillon); and former Mormon Robert McKay writes in *The Utah Evangel*, "And, if Mormon theology is correct, Mary was God's spirit-daughter begotten by Him in the pre-existence. Thus, if Mormon teachings are true, Jesus was begotten through an incestuous relationship!" McKay writes also, "If you think that the Mormon church is a Christian church, let me tell you as one who saw it from the inside, that Mormonism is in no way, shape or form Christian!"

What kind of strange powers did this man Joseph Smith have? What is the truth about the gold plates, the angelic visitation, and the strange doctrines of Mormonism?

Certainly this is not *all* of the "truth about Mormonism." But it is plenty. More can be learned by ordering the books or tracts listed at the end of this book.

In Utah, particularly, you feel the pressure of the Mormon church very strongly in almost every area of life and business. How did this vast part of America become so entrenched in the strange doctrines of Mormonism? We shall see!

—The Author

Foreword

It is an encouragement to those of us who plant churches in the West, particularly in Mormon areas, to be able to recommend Dr. Hugh Pyle's book, *The Truth About Mormonism.* A lot of material has been produced on this subject, but we feel that this book meets a real need.

First of all, Dr. Hugh Pyle has been in the West in evangelistic meetings. He does understand what it means to minister in Mormon country. Second, Pastor Harley Johnson and I have appreciated the openness of Brother Pyle to suggestions made by Harley Johnson and myself. Brother Johnson, the pastor of the Jordan Valley Baptist Church in West Jordan, Utah (Salt Lake area), is one of the most knowledgeable men on Mormonism today. He has discussed this subject with many, many LDS people and understands the thinking of the average LDS person.

Northwest Baptist Missions is an independent Baptist home mission agency that assists men in establishing fundamental Baptist churches in the Inter-Mountain West, particularly in Mormon cities and towns. We are glad to recommend this book to people in this area and to the Christian world.

This book is in touch with the reality of present-day Mormonism, and therefore we feel it will be valuable to Mormons and non-Mormons. May God greatly use this to cause people to pray for those who serve the Lord in this area, and to help us to understand the teachings of the Mormon church in comparison with the Scriptures.

Wallace W. Higgins,
Founder and Director of Northwest Baptist Missions,
Salt Lake City, Utah

Table of Contents

The Astounding Wealth and Growth of the Mormons

The income of the Mormon church is said to be $3½ million per day! It is listed in the top 50 corporations in America and is perhaps the fastest growing church among the major denominations in the country. Certainly it is one of the richest.

This is very impressive to the average citizen who doesn't know his Bible. Doesn't Marie Osmond belong to the Mormon church? (She is no longer an "Osmond." She's on her second husband!) How about Jake Garn, the first congressman to go into space? He is a Mormon. So also is the conservative Senator Orrin G. Hatch whom many evangelicals applaud. Former presidential candidate George Romney is Mormon as are the Marriott Hotel people. Last year the *New York Times Magazine* also reminded us that the president of the Public Broadcasting Service, the president of the University of California and the president of the General Mills Corporation are all Mormons! Now that's pretty impressive, isn't it?

Ezra Taft Benson, the present president of the Mormon church, was the U. S. Secretary of Agriculture under Eisenhower. He has inherited absolute authority over the Mormon church since he is the senior member of the Council of the Twelve Apostles which rules the church.

The *New York Times Magazine* for January 12, 1986, states that the Mormon church is enormously wealthy, richer probably than any other religious organization in the United States except the Roman Catholic Church. Its total assets are estimated at $8 billion and its yearly income at about $2 billion. About 75% of this comes from tithes and offerings. All Mormons are expected to tithe, no exceptions!

Besides temples and churches, the Mormons own television and radio stations, a daily newspaper, insurance companies, more than 800,000 acres of working farmland, industrial parks, several food processing plants, department stores, office buildings, real estate investments and stocks and bonds said to be worth hundreds of millions of dollars! Part of their commercial property includes about 60 acres in downtown Salt Lake City and a number of the buildings on this property. This is in addition to many ranches, book publishing businesses, malls, farms, and theme parks. And we haven't named them all!

Since money and possessions catch the attention of many people, it is not surprising that the Mormons have gained credibility they did not have before. Some say this wealthy religious giant was once just a hated and persecuted religious cult hunted down by federal marshalls because of their illegal polygamy (the practice of having more wives than one at a time), but is now a highly respected Christian denomination. Well, we shall see!

Certainly their great and lavish temples and the popular Mormon Tabernacle Choir would make the average Joe think well of them.

As for growth, the Mormons' birth rate is almost twice the national average, and the church is growing at a rate of almost 6% a year. Each and every day some 30,000 bicycle-riding, dark-suited young Mormon "missionaries" go out in a swarm to make more proselytes out of the unsuspecting public.

Worldwide membership at this writing (1987) has jumped 75% in the past twelve years to more than six million, including about two million overseas. New temples are opening up all over the world. They astound people with their magnificent architecture, the stunning gothic towers and sharply pointed steeples. Does such growth mean the Mormon church is of God?

2

Some Commendable Things About the Mormons

Salt Lake City is a clean and beautiful place. Almost everything the public sees is clean, modern and first-class in Mormon country. It all seems to smack of "success."

When I was in an Idaho town for a revival I visited a number of Mormon stores and shops. The clerks and salespeople were civil, some even friendly. Many of them took the salvation tracts I offered them.

Mormon missionaries are clean, well-groomed, polite and gracious. They are taught to be well-mannered and kind as they approach their prospective converts.

Many Mormons are hard-working, law-abiding, dedicated citizens. Most of them are conservative in politics. Some of our best and most worthy accomplishments in Washington have been aided by Mormon leaders.

The Central Intelligence Agency recruits heavily among young Mormons returning from missionary work abroad. Many Mormons also land jobs with the FBI.

Mormons give the impression they are great on education. Brigham Young University is a popular school with a football team that plays well with the best colleges in America.

Paula Hawkins, a Mormon, was a very popular U. S. Senator from Florida. She is gracious, sharp and talented. She has taken a good stand against abortion, pornography, child abuse, and other national evils.

THE TRUTH ABOUT MORMONISM

Mormons advertise in *Reader's Digest* with beautiful full-color displays to promote their beliefs in the traditional family and in what appears to be an earnest appeal to restore proper home life in America like it used to be.

This religion loudly announces its resistance to pornography, homosexuality, abortion, and women working outside the home.

Many Mormons have convictions about doing secular and worldly things on Sunday, putting some evangelical Christians to shame.

More and more prominent newspapers and magazines are giving space to commendable stories about the Mormons: their faith, their people, their wealth, their industry, their accomplishments, and much more. They emphasize their "strict standards," something these secular papers cannot say about a majority of churches and denominations that claim to be Christian. This to our shame!

Mormons are expected not to drink alcohol, smoke cigarettes, nor look at pornography. Even drinking coffee is off-limits to many of them. They think they'll do better here and in the hereafter because of such discipline.

The Mormon church claims to take good care of its "family." Partly from the tithes of its members the church keeps a vast storehouse of food and other commodities to help needy members. They own dairies and canneries. And the church offers a counseling service which helps keep troubled families under the watchful eye of the church. Mormon families are encouraged to work, and most of them prefer not to be on welfare. They want to work for what they get. The young are taught to be industrious.

The church teaches that homosexuality can be cured through fasting and prayer. They are correct in their belief that perverts are unnatural, and so unrepentant homosexuals are excommunicated. One such Mormon says the "church demands absolute conformity."

Mormons are zealous. In Craig, Colorado, for instance, a few Mormons have multiplied because of their missionary zeal, and now one out of every ten residents is a

Mormon! Emphasis in many western schools is put on sports; and where Mormons dominate, there are usually LDS coaches to indoctrinate their team members.

Mormons are making great strides now in Mexico, South and Central America, and the islands of the Pacific as well as in this country.

All of this reveals the tenacious zeal and the commendable virtues of this sect about which so little has been known until recently.

3

Does Mormonism Contradict the Bible?

This fast-growing religion is thought by many to be a Christian organization. People who do not know would assume that Mormons are biblical Christians with just a few minor differences. This is because they freely use the same terms that Christians use. On every subject except religion, Mormons use the same definitions for their words as the rest of the English-speaking world. But when it comes to spiritual matters, Mormons have developed a completely different dictionary for their vocabulary.

One of the biggest problems faced by Christians when talking to Mormons is being able to explain what we believe in terms that they will understand. Mormons use the same words we use, but they have entirely different meanings. When Mormons talk about being "born again," they are thinking of baptism into the LDS Church. To a Mormon the "Gospel" is the Mormon church system and teachings. "Heaven," to the Mormon, is divided into three kingdoms: celestial, terrestrial and telestial. Your works and whether you join the Mormon church determine to which kingdom you will go. To them "eternal life" is exaltation in their highest (celestial) kingdom where they will be producing children through the sexual union of husbands and wives who were married in a Mormon temple. For the Mormon, "Hell" is a prison where the inmates come and go. People stay only until their debt has been paid to God.

There is no term that means the same to the Mormon

9

as it means to the Bible-believing Christian. When talking with a Mormon, we need to define every word!

Now let's see if Mormonism contradicts God's Word, the Bible. Keep in mind that "all scripture is given by inspiration of God" (II Tim. 3:16). God says that "holy men of God spake as they were moved by the Holy Ghost" (II Pet. 1:21) in writing the Bible and that the Word does not come by any private interpretation (II Pet. 1:20). Isaiah said, "...the word of our God shall stand for ever" (Isa. 40:8).

Not only does God say that the Bible is the Word of God, but Jesus (God the Son) reiterated when He cried, "Heaven and earth shall pass away, but my words shall not pass away" (Matt. 24:35).

Not only did God the Father and God the Son declare that the Bible was THE Word of God, but the prophets believed it (Isa. 40:8; Jer. 23:16, 28, 29). The apostles declared it (Eph. 6:17; II Tim. 3:16; Col. 3:16). David, the man after God's own heart, surely believed that God's Word was not only superior but that it is final (Ps. 119:89, 90)!

The Bible is proven to be the Word of God by its amazing unity, by its depth, by its influence, and by its preservation through the centuries. It is also proven to be the Word of God by the astounding fulfillment of its prophecies.

Not only that, but the Bible surely is revealed as the Word of God by the amazing transformation in the lives of those who have accepted its plan of salvation and adopted its truths to live by!

There are many other proofs that the Bible is God's Word, too numerous to mention, and this is important when we read the warnings which God gives throughout both the Old and the New Testaments. Deuteronomy 4:2 warns the nation of Israel against adding to or diminishing from the commandments of the Lord your God (Deut. 12:32 and Prov. 30:6). In the last warning which God sounds in this marvelous and amazing Book, He declares that the man who tampers with it, adds to or takes away from the words of the book of this prophecy not only will have terrible plagues added to him, but God will take away his part out of the book of life (Rev. 22:18, 19).

The Word of the Lord is perfect and complete (I Cor. 13:10; Ps. 19:7). It is impossible to improve on perfection! Psalm 19 also tells us that the Word of God is sure, right, pure, clean and enduring (vss. 7–9).

With this in mind, let us compare what the Bible teaches and what Mormonism teaches. The contradictions are immediately evident!

Is God an Exalted Man?

Mormonism says that "God himself was once as we are now, and is an exalted man" (*Teachings of the Prophet Joseph Smith,* p. 345). They also say that "The Father has a body of flesh and bones as tangible as man's" (*Doctrine and Covenants,* 130:22).

The Bible teaches that "God is the infinite and perfect Spirit in whom all things have their source, support, and end."—Strong, an eminent theologian.

God is self-existent, a Spirit eternal, unchanging; and He formed man out of the dust of the ground (John 4:24; Ps. 90:2; Mal. 3:6; Gen. 2:7).

Joseph Smith said, "You have got to learn how to be Gods yourselves, and to be kings and priests to God, the same as all Gods have done before you..." (*King Follett Discourse,* p. 10).

But God in the Bible says that those who receive Christ thus become the sons of God (John 1:12) and that there is one God and one Mediator between God and man, even Christ Jesus (I Tim. 2:5)!

Mormonism says that, "if it had not been for Joseph Smith and the restoration there would be no salvation. There is no salvation outside the Church of Jesus Christ of Latter Day Saints" (*Mormon Doctrine,* p. 670).

God, of course, declares that we are saved by grace through faith in the finished work of Christ (Eph. 2:8) and

11

that "it is...not of works" (Eph. 2:9; Rom. 4:5)!

Was Adam's Fall Into Sin a Blessing?

Mormonism says: "And now behold, if Adam had not transgressed he would not have fallen—And they would have had no children...Adam fell that men might be; and men are, that they might have joy" (*Book of Mormon*, 2 Nephi 2:22, 23, 25).

Mormon "Apostle" Bruce R. McConkie explains: "Properly understood, it becomes apparent that the fall of Adam is one of the greatest blessings ever given of God to mankind" (*A New Witness for the Articles of Faith*, p. 87).

The Bible teaches that sin is rebellion against God, a transgression of His law. Sin is what separates man from his Creator. To fully understand the seriousness of sin, it is necessary to understand what had to be done to bring God and man together. The Lord Jesus, who was without sin, went to the cross where He suffered and died to reconcile sinful men to a righteous and holy God (I John 3:4; Isa. 59:2; Heb. 4:15; Rom. 5:10; II Cor. 5:18–20).

Do the Mormons Have the Gospel?

Mormonism says: "The true gospel of Jesus Christ was restored to earth in the last days through the instrumentality of Joseph Smith. It is found only in The Church of Jesus Christ of Latter-day Saints" (*Mormon Doctrine*, by McConkie, p. 334).

This Mormon general authority also says of the "gospel," "It embraces all of the laws, principles, doctrines, rites, ordinances, acts, powers, authorities, and keys necessary to save and exalt men in the highest heaven hereafter" (*Ibid.*, p. 331).

To further enlighten us, McConkie says: "Indeed, the very possession of the fulness of the everlasting gospel consists in having the Melchizedek Priesthood and the gift of the Holy Ghost" (*A New Witness for the Articles of Faith*, p. 142).

The Bible teaches that the Gospel is the Good News that Christ died to pay the penalty for this sin-stained, Hell-bound, ungodly human race that has turned its back on God; that after His death on the cross of Calvary Christ was buried; then He rose from the dead the third day. We see this biblical Gospel at work when people are saved by believing on the Lord Jesus Christ just like the Philippian jailer Paul and Silas won (I Cor. 15:1–4; Acts 16:30, 31).

Are Sinners Cleansed by Fire?

Joseph Fielding Smith, who became president of the Mormon church, said: "...we must receive the gift of the Holy Ghost; we must be born again; we must have sin and iniquity burned out of our souls as though by fire; we must gain a new creation by the power of the Holy Ghost" (*British Area General Conference Report*, Aug. 1971, p. 54).

Delbert L. Stapley said: "Man can only become spotless and sanctified by the reception of the Holy Ghost in his personal life. The Holy Ghost is a cleansing and purifying agent to all who receive it and are righteous. This means that sin and iniquity are spiritually burned out of the repentant person. He then receives a remission of sins, and his soul is sanctified and made clean for the Holy Ghost to abide in him" (*Conference Report*, Oct. 1966, p. 112).

Mormon Apostle Bruce R. McConkie explained how all this was supposed to take place. "After baptism in water, legal administrators lay their hands upon a repentant person and say: 'Receive the Holy Ghost.' This gives him the gift of the Holy Ghost, which is the right to the constant companionship of that member of the Godhead based on faithfulness. Either then or later, depending upon the individual's personal worthiness, the Holy Ghost comes. The baptized person becomes a new creature. He is baptized with fire, sin and evil are burned out of his soul, and he is born again" (*A New Witness for the Articles of Faith*, p. 291).

The Bible in no place teaches that sin and iniquity are burned out of the soul by the Holy Ghost. God has always

THE TRUTH ABOUT MORMONISM

used BLOOD as the agent for cleansing. The Old Testament blood sacrifices were all pointing to man's need of cleansing; but it is not possible for the blood of animal sacrifices to take away the sins of mankind. God sent His Son into this world to shed His precious blood for the cleansing of man's sin. It is the blood of Jesus Christ, God's Son, that cleanseth us from all sin (Lev. 17:11; Heb. 9:18–22; 10:4; I John 1:7; Rev. 1:5).

Baptized for the Dead?

Mormonism teaches that a person in the Mormon church can be baptized for some dead one who has gone on before and thus place him in the Mormon church and help save his soul.

God says, "It is appointed unto men once to die, but after this the judgment" (Heb. 9:27). "How shall we escape, if we neglect so great salvation?" (Heb. 2:3); and the Bible emphasizes, "NOW is the accepted time; behold, now is the day of salvation" (II Cor. 6:2).

Mormonism slurs the Christian church and its ordinances and often declares that all churches are wrong while only Mormonism has the "true gospel." The Bible declares that Christ founded the church and said the gates of Hell will not prevail against it (Matt. 16:18). He purchased the church with His own blood (Acts 20:28).

Distortion of the Bible

Mormons use the Bible only as far as they can make it fit in with their heresy. They say the Bible is the Word of God "only as translated correctly" (by them)! No Romanist, Campbellite or Jehovah's Witness was ever more deceptive!

Mormonism says, "Some degree of salvation will come to all who have not forfeited their right to it" (*Articles of Faith*, p. 91). "The great punishment of those who have done evil will be that they have failed to achieve all that was within their possibilities" (Mormon paper, *Life's Meaning*).

14

But the *Bible* says that it is either Heaven or Hell, that men are either saved or lost, that the unsaved will "have no rest day nor night," but are tormented, and that "the smoke of their torment ascendeth up for ever and ever" (Rev. 14:11), that the lost go to "the lake which burneth with fire and brimstone: which is the second death" (21:8).

Mormonism accepts the Bible, plus the *Book of Mormon,* plus the *Book of Doctrine and Covenants,* plus their *Pearl of Great Price,* plus what their prophet says, all as the Word of God; but the Bible is God's Word *only* "as properly interpreted" (by them)! *God* tells us that the Word of God is sufficient for man and says, "Add thou not unto his words, lest he reprove thee, and thou be found a liar" (Prov. 30:6).

These are just a very few of the many, many great truths of the Bible that Mormonism denies and for which it substitutes its own fanciful and unscriptural ideas. They claim to be Christians, but it is doubtful if there is a cult on earth that is any further astray from the truth! The next chapters will help us to see why.

4

The Mormon Murder Mystery

The Mormon students and writers (as well as secular investigators) have been recently looking into the origins and the hidden mysteries of the Mormon religion. Until now if anyone dared to question the *Book of Mormon* or the background of Joseph Smith or the many wives of Brigham Young, they were usually silenced by the towering Mormon officials, or it is believed by some that they were bought off in one way or another.

Recently, however, some documents have surfaced that seem to place in doubt some of the Mormon church's fundamental teachings. Two Mormons involved in the search for documents about Mormonism have been murdered.

To make matters worse for them, there has been an increase of missionary work by worthy and dedicated Christians who are making real inroads into Mormon territory and opening the eyes of some of Joseph Smith's followers. Ex-Mormons have produced a motion picture called "The God Makers" which assails the Church of Jesus Christ of Latter-day Saints as "one of the most dangerous and deceptive groups in the world." The film shows it to be a rich cult that dabbles in pagan practices and the occult, distorting its history and brainwashing its members.

Jews are upset about plans for a Mormon branch of Brigham Young University in Jerusalem, and orthodox Christian denominations are branding the Mormons as an "unchristian cult." Still, there are many who are being deceived. Norman Vincent Peale acclaimed a former Mormon president as a "great man of God," and Southern Baptist Baylor University for some time now has had a Mormon professor teaching there!

In 1909 one of the church's respected historians wrote (as quoted in the *New York Times Magazine*), "If the origin of the *Book of Mormon* could be proved to be other than that set forth by Joseph Smith...then the Church of Jesus Christ of Latter-day Saints, and its message and doctrines, which in some respects may be said to have arisen out of the *Book of Mormon,* must fall."

Other challenges to Mormon history and doctrine have come from historians who can find no evidence to support their teaching that early American Indians were really Jews who had come to this land long ago, as their cluttered and contradictory *Book of Mormon* teaches.

The greatest challenges have recently come from within the Mormon church itself. This, apparently, they will not tolerate. One such writer has revealed that the *Book of Mormon* is remarkably similar to another book, *View of the Hebrews,* written in 1823 by a Christian minister, Ethan Smith. He pointed out many similarities, coincidences, and identical language in the two volumes. This led to his assertion that Joseph Smith had fabricated the *Book of Mormon.*

A letter written by Smith seems to be obsessed with finding buried treasure guarded by "spirits." The letter lends some credence to church critics who claim Smith was an imaginative dabbler in folk magic, according to Robert Lindsey in the *New York Times* expose'. It seems that Mormonism can always easily explain any such thing away. A few words from the present prophet and President of the LDS Church is enough to keep gullible cult members in blissful ignorance and submission.

Close the Vaults!

In the early eighties Mormon elders ordered the closing of certain church archives to scholars they felt to be unfriendly. Too many things were coming to light. Members of the church historical team were especially warned not to publish works on polygamy or other Mormon peculiarities that might prove embarrassing. More and more such stories or reports had to be carefully laundered. It is said that one scholar who proved that much of the *Book of Mormon* had been stolen from the King James Bible was forced from his job and now has a different position!

A strong warning was sounded just over a year ago by a Mormon apostle who declared that those who dared to question the official accounts of Joseph Smith or his successors or to challenge the "settled, fundamental doctrines of the church" would do so at "spiritual peril."

On October 15, 1985, Steven Christiansen, a 31-year-old investment counselor and Mormon bishop, who had donated a questionable old letter to the Mormon church, arrived at his sixth floor office in the Judge Building, a few blocks from Temple Square. He leaned over to pick up a package addressed to him. It exploded, hurling his body through the door riddled with hardened-steel nails. That same morning a woman whose husband had helped Christiansen with that letter picked up a package at her suburban Salt Lake City home and was instantly killed when it exploded.

A Mark Hoffman has since confessed to the murders after several months of puzzling investigation. Hoffman and Christiansen are said to have been working together to purchase a set of documents from the early days of the Mormon church. These letters were supposed to contain damaging comments about Joseph Smith and Mormonism. Many rumors have abounded.

Questions remain. Why was the Latter-day Saints Church dealing with Hoffman? What did they want to hide? Are they running scared?

Why does the Mormon church resist so fervently any investigation into or revelation of the truth about Joseph Smith and the origin of the *Book of Mormon?* I am reminded of what an undertaker once told me a Catholic priest said. It seems the priest spent so much time with the communion wine that he frequently had to be sobered up before he could even halfway stand to conduct a funeral. One time when he was still pretty much under the influence, he blurted out, "Keep 'em ignorant and keep 'em superstitious, and you can keep 'em Catholic." Apparently the same could be said of the Mormon devotees.

5

Water on the Brain

Almost every false religion makes baptism a part of their spurious plan of "salvation." Whether they immerse like the Campbellites (Church of Christ) or sprinkle like the Catholics, they feel a strong imperative to seal the "convert's" entrance into their church (and thus into Heaven) with water. While Baptists and other Christians may be justified in calling Campbellites "water bugs" (as some do), we will have to admit that they would be hard pressed to outstrip (or out-water) the Mormons!

This false teaching of salvation by water is listed in most books on the cults. One would imagine that they take a good verse like Titus 3:5 which reads, "Not by works of righteousness which we have done, but according to his mercy he saved us, by the washing of regeneration, and renewing of the Holy Ghost," and attempt to read baptism into the "washing."

One does not have to look far in the Bible, however, to discern that our sins are remitted in the blood of Christ, "in whom we have redemption through his blood" (Eph. 1:7), and "ye know that ye were not redeemed with corruptible things...But with the precious blood of Christ" (I Pet. 1:18, 19).

Furthermore, John clinches it in the final book (Revelation) by announcing that Christ "loved us, and *washed* us from our sins in his own blood" (Rev. 1:5). So the "washing of regeneration" is certainly not water baptism! See my book, *The Truth About the Church of Christ,* published by Sword of the Lord Publishers for a fuller treatment on the water-baptism-for-salvation teaching.

Mormon president Charles W. Penrose wrote, "Not a soul can enter into the kingdom of God unless he or she is a true believer in Jesus Christ and has been born of the water and the Spirit. Even Christ was born of water in his burial by baptism in Jordan and His coming forth from the womb of waters. He was the example for mankind. This is the straight and narrow way."

So, according to Mormon teaching, the straight and narrow way is to be baptized, and, of course, by a qualified Mormon (above quote from *Rays of Living Light,* page 37, by Penrose)! Other Mormon writings and tracts emphasize the need for water baptism to assist in washing away sins. The *Book of Mormon* has a third more references to baptism than all of the Bible has!

They have so much water on the brain that they even baptize people for others who have previously died. Floyd McElveen in his excellent book, *Will the Saints Go Marching In?* states,

"The real purpose of all Mormon genealogical work is to provide information for baptizing for the dead, proxy sealing ordinances (an ordinance whereby husbands and wives are sealed together in the marriage union for time and eternity), and ordination and endowments for dead relatives to help save or exalt them."

Roman Catholics collect money from deluded and grieving relatives for loved ones who have died to supposedly get them out of a purgatory that never existed, while Mormons actually dupe their blinded members into thinking they can save a dead friend or relative by getting in the water for him!

McElveen continues, "Thus Mormons search out the names of the dead through genealogical research and proceed to be baptized in their behalf. President Joseph Fielding Smith said, "The greatest commandment given us, and made obligatory, is the temple work in our own behalf and in behalf of our dead."

Anyone who is depending on water baptism to save him is, of course, not depending on the grace of God and the blood of Christ to save him. Penrose, in *What the Mormons Believe*, states, "Repentance leads to remission of sins, which comes through baptism administered by one having authority," etc. "He is brought forth from the womb of waters, thus being born of water to a new life in Christ Jesus. Born of the water and of the Spirit the regenerated soul becomes a member of Christ's church." (Campbellites and Catholics would say the same thing, each claiming to be Christ's church.)

Penrose the Mormon continues, "Faith, repentance and baptism of water and of the Spirit administered by divine authority are essential to salvation." And later, "The living may be baptized for the dead. One who has received the ordinances can stand proxy for departed ancestors" (*What the Mormons Believe*, by Penrose).

To convince their people that they can be baptized for lost loved ones who have already died thus ties the deceived Mormon even more closely to the cult since most people feel a great burden to do something to help their departed relatives. It is a wonder the Roman Catholics didn't think of this first! One thing sure, they never got the idea from the Bible!

Bible-believing Christians know that baptism is an outward expression of an in-worked salvation. We are baptized because we have been saved, not in order to be saved. "When they believed...they were baptized" (Acts 8:12). Baptism identifies the newborn soul with the death, burial and resurrection of Christ. It is putting on the uniform of Christ. It is pleasing to God, but it is certainly not the means of salvation. Salvation is by grace through faith in the finished work of Christ (Eph. 2:8, 9). "The blood of Jesus Christ his Son cleanseth us from all sin" (I John 1:7)!

6

Joseph Smith and His Magic Goggles

Or, Where Did the *Book of Mormon* Come From?

Ezra Benson called the *Book of Mormon* "the most correct book on earth." If he really believes that, then he must be the most deceived man on earth!

Many Mormon leaders feel, I am sure, that Mormonism stands or falls on the accuracy of the *Book of Mormon*. When I read what so many critics of the *Book of Mormon* said about it, I wondered why on earth do not Mormons really wade into it and find out for themselves what it really is. But then I read it for myself, and I'm sure I know at least one good reason why, for the *Book of Mormon* is about the driest and dullest book imaginable. Full of repetition and contradiction, it is a hodgepodge of words taken from many sources. It would take a strange mind, indeed, to make sense of it. Chapter after chapter is given to wars between people no one ever heard of or ever has heard of since. Then right in the midst of all this journey through boredom, a few verses from the New Testament will be inserted. Every now and then, to add bulk and authority to the book, one will find whole chapters taken from the Old Testament.

Chapters and verses will be inserted sometimes from the Old and then from the New Testaments without rhyme or reason. As one has commented, it has to be one of the most boring pieces of literature ever written. Thus, there is not much danger that very many people will read very far in it!

Missionary Harley Johnson writes, "The danger lies in that those who are considering joining the Mormons will believe that the doctrines taught in the *Book of Mormon* are the doctrines of Mormonism. The *Book of Mormon* teaches very little Mormon doctrine. To find the doctrines of Mormonism, one must read their books, *Doctrines and Covenants, Pearl of Great Price,* and study the teachings of the general authorities of their church."

Joseph Smith claims that when he was a young boy he was visited by an angel named Moroni who told him to dig up some hidden gold plates from a hillside in New York State. Moroni is supposed to have previously been the son of a man named Mormon long before. After these annual trips to the hill to view his find, he was finally told by the angel that he could read the gold plates and interpret what they said with the aid of some looking glasses called the Urim and Thummim. These words, too, he copied from the Bible.

History proves that Smith was always delving into mysterious and hidden things. He was convicted of being a "glass looker," like a fortuneteller gazing into a crystal ball.

Yet, strangely, Mormon apostle and leader David O. McKay stated, "The appearing of the Father and the Son to Joseph Smith is the foundation of this church." Joseph Smith at 17 did not even know whether there was a Supreme Being even though Mormon leaders say he was "visited by God" at 14. Floyd McElveen in his book on the saints gives much historical evidence that Joseph Smith was a false prophet. God had warned the human race already about such; for He says in Matthew 24:11, "And many false prophets shall rise, and shall deceive many." And again in II Corinthians 11:13–15, "For such are false apostles, deceitful workers....Satan himself is transformed into an angel of light....his ministers also," etc.

How do we know that Joseph Smith is a false prophet? Because what he claimed to see and hear is in contradiction to the Word of God. God says, "If they speak not according to this word, it is because there is no light in them" (Isa. 8:20).

The lad who was so interested in looking for buried treasure used his alleged psychic ability by telling fortunes and finding lost things with his peep stone. His father testified to the fact that young Joseph could put his peep stone into a hat and tell people where to find hidden things. Not many years later he started the Church of Jesus Christ of Latter-day Saints. He claimed that God told him he was to "restore" the church that had been defunct for centuries. Thus it was to be the Church of "Latter-day Saints."

The Mormon Migration

The *Book of Mormon* claims that a people called the Jaredites, refugees from the Tower of Babel, migrated to America about 2247 B.C. They lived in Central America until they died out because of internal strife. One survivor, "Ether," recorded the history on metallic plates. Then about 600 B.C. two families of Lehi and Ishmael left Jerusalem, crossed the Pacific, and landed in South America.

Much of the *Book of Mormon* is made up of wars between the "Lamanites" and the "Nephites." They say God put a curse on the Lamanites and made their skins dark and so they became the American Indians! God, they say, favored the Nephites; so just after He was crucified, Jesus is supposed to have come over here and instituted baptism by immersion, the sacrament of bread and wine, the priesthood and other teachings. The Commander-in-Chief of the Nephites was named Mormon who, when he saw that the Lamanites had killed off all of the "good guys" (the Nephites) wrote the famous gold plates for Joseph Smith to find many centuries later.

When Columbus landed in 1492, the infidel Lamanites were supposed to have by then become American Indians instead of Jews! Mormon's son Moroni, who later became an angel, supposedly traveled clear across the country from the Southwest, over 2,000 miles, carrying the "gold plates" which would have weighed over 200 pounds!

In New York State he supposedly buried the plates so young Joseph Smith, the would-be fortune-teller, could find them with his magic goggles or "peep stones." The goggles were supposed to have been a large pair of spectacles which Smith called the Urim and the Thummim. Mormon was supposed to have written his gold plate special in "reformed Egyptian."

If you are willing to believe all of the above, you could just as easily believe in the tooth fairy and that the Easter bunny lays colored eggs in April. Also I would like to sell you the Brooklyn Bridge and some swamp land in Florida!

History, anthropology and archaeology all contradict the tale of the Mormon plates. They can find no "reformed Egyptian" language; and, anyway, no Jews would be caught dead putting sacred writings into the (hated) Egyptian if they wanted to!

Furthermore, the American Indians have skin and characteristics which identify them with the Asians, not Europeans. It is believed by anthropologists that they came over through the Bering Straits into Alaska and down, rather than somehow making it across the Atlantic or Pacific and settling in South and Central America.

Joseph Fielding Smith, past president of the Mormon church, stated, "Mormonism must stand or fall on the story of Joseph Smith. He was either a prophet of God, divinely called, properly appointed and commissioned, or he was one of the biggest frauds this world has ever seen. There is no middle ground" (*Doctrines of Salvation*, p. 188).

Well put! Surely intelligent, college-trained and successful businessmen today know that Smith was a phony if they have looked into the matter at all. Why, then, do they remain in the Mormon church and go along with all the ceremony and trappings that perpetrate such a fraud? There could be several reasons:

For one thing, human nature hates to admit it is wrong

or has been deceived. Pride just won't let them admit it. A lust for and craving for power, too, must affect some of the men who have great places of honor in the Mormon leadership with thousands of people looking up to them. Thus some would go along with the big fraud just as others might like to become Worshipful Master of his lodge or the governor of his state or top kingpin in the Mafia.

Missionary Harley Johnson reminds us of two other major reasons some remain in Mormonism: *tradition,* which includes looking back to the sufferings of early Mormons as they moved from place to place, finally making the arduous trip west to the Salt Lake Valley; and *church organization,* which involves every member in the program of the Mormon church.

Remember, too, that Satan is an arch fiend and the great deceiver. He hates God and the Bible and has control over all religions and religious leaders who are not saved men, indwelt by the Holy Spirit, serving God in a scriptural manner.

Finally, "the love of money is the root of all evil," the Bible asserts; and very few who are getting rich in a multi-million-dollar religious scam want to kill the goose that keeps laying the golden eggs!

Joseph Smith certainly did find the gold for modern-day successors among his "latter-day saints." Hal Mason of Baptist Mid-Missions writes, "The president of the Mormon church today knows that Joseph Smith's first vision was a fraud and all that came from the vision is a fraud." Mormon leaders have suppressed this for years, but Jerald and Sandra Tanner have written details of letters and statements which prove that they know it.

Mason concludes, "The president of the Mormon church continues this fraud in order to protect the over three-million-dollar-per-day income. When a man has sold his soul to Satan for worldly gain, there is no limit to the villainous depredation he will visit upon the innocent and unaware. Such is the history of Joseph Smith and those who follow him."

7

Mormonism Blasphemes Jesus

Mormons place no more value upon the blood of Jesus than they do on the blood of Joseph Smith. I have before me the copy of a Mormon Sunday school lesson in which Jesus and Joseph Smith are compared, side by side. The lesson claims that Joseph, like Jesus, was born of humble parentage. Each heard the voice of God appointing him (though Joseph Smith had no witnesses of this!). Jesus was baptized by John the Baptist; Joseph Smith had a special appearance from John the Baptist who baptized him and conferred the Aaronic priesthood upon him (again no witnesses!). Christ healed the sick and conferred this power upon His disciples; Joe Smith was supposed to have done the same! Jesus was persecuted; Smith was persecuted. Jesus shed His blood; Smith sealed his testimony with his blood, etc.

Charles Penrose in *Blood Atonement* states that an adulterer or a murderer could not be saved by Christ's blood but, if their throats were cut by the authorities of the church, they could receive remission of sins by their own blood!

Joseph Fielding Smith (*Doctrines of Salvation*, Vol. 2, pp. 133, 134) writes: "Those who live lives of wickedness may also be heirs of salvation—that is, they too shall be redeemed from death and from hell eventually. These, however, must suffer in hell the torments of the damned until they pay the price of their sinning, for the blood of Christ will not cleanse them." What terrible heresy and blasphemy!

"Christ's atonement was not sufficient for personal sins" (James Talmage, *The Articles of Faith*).

Jesus Was Married?

"Jesus was married at Cana to the Marys and Martha whereby he could see his seed before he was crucified." "Christ was a descendant of David by plural wife Bathsheba, and if David had not been a polygamist there would have been no redeemer." (These quotes from Parley Pratt, *Key to the Science of Theology,* Brigham Young in *Journal of Discourses,* and Richards in *Millennial Star*).

When my wife and I several years ago entered the Visitors' Center at the main Mormon Tabernacle in Salt Lake City, we saw an altar which had an offering of fruit and vegetables upon it with Adam and Eve kneeling at each side. A lamb lies by its side—*alive*. This is Cain's altar which was rejected by God in the Bible. But the Mormons by placing Cain's altar there have gone on record as preferring the bloodless offering of Cain to the lamb of Abel. The lamb slain is what God calls for as it points forward to the blood of Christ offered on the cross—which blood the Mormon church despises!

NOTE: In 1986 Cain's altar was replaced by a statue of Adam and Eve standing next to each other with no altar at all.

Not only do they play down the value of the blood of the divine Saviour, but they reduce Emmanuel to mere "man." And an adulterous man at that! They teach, "We say that it was Jesus Christ who was married (at Cana) to the Marys and Martha" (*Journal of Discourses,* Vol. 2, p. 80). "Now let us inquire concerning the wives of Jesus; There were several holy women who greatly loved Jesus and when he arose from the dead he appeared first to these women or at least one of them, Mary Magdalene. Now it would be very natural for a husband in the resurrection to appear first to his own dear wives" (*The Seer,* p. 159). How absurd, blasphemous, and utterly unscriptural can you get!

In *Journal of Discourses,* Vol. 4, p. 259, the blasphemy is even more pronounced, for there the Mormons teach that Jesus was quite intimate with the women and that, if He had not been married to them, His actions would have been improper and unbecoming and that, if He had not been married, He would have been tarred and feathered. This alone ought to be enough to utterly nauseate any person who has ever read the Bible or knows anything at all about the glorious Person of the sinless Saviour, God the Son! Any Mormon with an ounce of morality should immediately renounce this monstrous false religion!

Men who imagine the Saviour to be less than holy God usually also imagine all preachers to be women-grabbing, harlot-hungry fornicators. Men who think that low are, of course, already in the gutter themselves. Is it any wonder, then, that Joseph Smith taught polygamy and that Brigham Young, his noted successor, had at least 27 wives? Some say Joseph Smith had 48 wives! Jesus said, "A corrupt tree bringeth forth evil fruit" (Matt. 7:17). No wonder such evil men produced such a crooked and perverse religion!

8

How Many Wives Does a Man Need?

Almost all of the Mormon apostles, bishops, and priests had plural wives (harems, or women living in various places) until the federal government passed a law banning polygamy in 1882. Mormons would not stop the evil practice until 1889 when they were convicted in federal courts. Joseph Smith had died many years earlier (June 27, 1844) after teaching and practicing polygamy. No wonder the lynch mob was determined to kill this adulterous woman-chaser.

When the president of the Mormon church in 1890 told the Mormon men they'd have to quit having so many wives, the idea was adopted as a "revelation," but they never slowed down until they were forced to by law. Many of them, it is believed, still practice plural wives.

The Church of Jesus Christ of Latter-day Saints with headquarters in Salt Lake City, officially, no longer accepts polygamy. There are, however, several off-shoot groups who believe the doctrine of plural wives was given by God (*Doctrines and Covenants*, Sec. 132:61–66) and continue in this practice.

In *The Good News Broadcaster* for June, 1986, the story is told of Colorado City, Arizona where Daniel Barlow, the town's first mayor who serves on the school board, has five wives! The desert town is largely owned by a cooperative religious trust, controlled by a Mormon group. For a half century it has been known as a haven for polygamists. It is located near the Utah state line. Originally the town was built on skids and could be towed across the state line in case of raids by Arizona officials. Most Utah officials are Mormons, no doubt! The town is hard to get to from the rest of Arizona since it is cut off by the Grand Canyon. School children comprise nearly half of the population. I guess so. One town elder has reportedly fathered 80 of those children! The town's founder, "Uncle Roy" Leroy Johnson, had married 16 wives before he died at 98. So at heart Mormons haven't changed.

It is easy to see why Mormons have little real use for the Bible except as a crutch or a filler for their own shallow writings. For in I Timothy 3 God declares that a bishop or elder must be "the husband of one wife." To even look and lust after another woman is to be guilty of adultery, the Saviour taught.

Van Baalen in *The Gist of the Cults* reminds us that Mormons quit having plural wives only because they had to and that the Mormon missionaries (many of them) when pressed will still admit that they believe in it but they don't practice it. Of course, they don't practice it because they would fear ending up in prison if they did. How many of them have several women is not known. In most places they do not publicly admit to having more than one wife at a time. But they still believe in polygamy because Mormon doctrine has taught it. They also teach that they will continue to have bodies of flesh and blood, will still have sex and still bear children in the life beyond.

Van Baalen says they believe they will populate the stars with their offspring. Mormon women would rather be part of a Mormon man's harem here than not be married at all, for they are taught that, if they are not married, they cannot reign in Heaven with their men but could only occupy the role of a servant.

9

How'd You Like to Become a God?

It matters not to Mormons that the Bible teaches there is "one God." They have gods all over the place and more to come. One of the enticing lies of Mormonism is the same one the Devil uttered in the Garden of Eden, "...your eyes shall be opened, and ye shall be as gods, knowing good and evil" (Gen. 3:5).

Satan wanted to be like God or wanted to be equal to God. "I will be like the most high," he said in Isaiah 14:14. Joseph Smith also had the same great ambition. The idea of being God had always fascinated him, so it is no wonder that he incorporated the idea into his new religion. Guess who Smith was running with when he thought of that? Mr. Satan himself first invented the notion!

Joseph Smith taught, "You have got to learn to be Gods yourselves; to be kings and priests to God, the same as all Gods have done" (*The King Follett Discourse*, pp. 10, 11). He also taught, "There is a God above the Father of our Lord Jesus Christ" (*Mormon Doctrine*, pp. 322, 323).

In their *Articles of Faith,* Mormons read, "We believe in a God who is Himself progressive...a being who has attained his exalted state, a path which now his children are permitted to follow....As man is, God once was; As God is, man may be."

It does not bother these cultists that God in the Bible says, "Before me there was no God formed, neither shall there be after me" (Isa. 43:10). Again in Isaiah 44:6, "Thus saith the Lord...the Lord of hosts; I am the first, and I am the last; and beside me there is no God." Many, many other verses prove the same thing. There is *one* God. All others are false gods!

Mormonism teaches "both the Father and the Son, as also all exalted beings, are now or in due course will become Gods of Gods" ("Teachings," pp. 343-376 in *Mormon Doctrine,* compiled by Bruce R. McConkie). "A plurality of Gods exists...there is an infinite number of holy personages, drawn from worlds without number, who have passed on to exaltation and are thus Gods" (pp. 576, 577). And again: "Godhood is not for men only; it is for men and women together" (p. 844).

Brigham Young said in *Journal of Discourses,* "If I am faithful with yourselves, that I shall see the time with yourselves that we shall know how to prepare to organize an earth like this—know how to people that earth, how to redeem it, how to sanctify it, and how to glorify it, with those who live upon it."

Well, that ought to settle it: if you believe such utter nonsense as this, you have to completely deny all that God has ever revealed in His wonderful Word, the Bible! Which will you believe?

NOTE: While we cannot become gods—nor should we want to—we can truly become the children of God through faith in the remarkable redemption of Christ on the cross and His glorious resurrection from the tomb (John 1:12, Gal. 3:26). Then one day we will give glory to God for sending His Son, "For of him, and through him, and to him, are all things: to whom be glory for ever. Amen" (Rom. 11:36).

10

What Is the *Book of Mormon?*
Why It Could Not Be the Word of God

Joseph Smith claims the *Book of Mormon* was a translation from the gold plates he dug up in a New York hillside as a boy. One who has read the Bible for many years (I have studied it for 50 years and preached it for 47 years) has an eerie feeling when reading something like this. It does not have the same spirit or "ring" at all that the Bible does! It is not intelligent, it is not helpful, it is not comforting, it is not encouraging.

There is all the difference in the world between God's Word, the Bible, and this fabricated *Book of Mormon* so-called. The Bible begins, "In the beginning." It explains God's dealings with man through the ages, has as its central message the Person and work of Jesus Christ, and concludes with the end of all things. The *Book of Mormon* does none of these.

The Bible has beauty, warmth, love, grace. The mark of true divinity is all through it. The *Book of Mormon* is just the opposite. The only part of the *Book of Mormon* that is at all encouraging or enlightening is the verses that have been taken from their context and snitched from the Bible.

Stealing the King James

To give the *Book of Mormon* some strength and luster, Smith took many chapters from the Bible and inserted them in his book. If he had been using them in an intelligent way to glorify God and had admitted that he got them from the Bible, it wouldn't have been quite so bad. But they are inserted just as if the "angel" Moroni had actually inspired and written them for the occasion.

The chapters and verses are from the King James Bible exactly. It is very interesting how Mormon or Moroni was supposed to have the King James Bible at hand even though it was not translated from Hebrew and Greek until A.D. 1611, more than 1,000 years after Mormon and Moroni were supposed to have lived! How does Joseph Smith think we are supposed to have confidence in his tale about the buried plates that were supposed to have contained the King James hundreds of years before it came into existence?

Further, God would not inspire a book that contradicted exactly what He had taught in the Word of God. An intelligent God would not teach baptismal regeneration in the *Book of Mormon* and salvation by grace through faith in the Bible. He would not magnify the blood of His Son in the Bible and teach the opposite in another book. For instance, teaching salvation by works in 2 Nephi 25:23 where the *Book of Mormon* says, "It is by grace we are saved, after all we can do!"

The Bible says that God has magnified His Word even above His name (Ps. 138:2). But Mormonism in the *Book of Mormon* ridicules the idea of so honoring the Bible: "And because my words shall hiss forth ["hiss" is a good word for them—the hiss of the serpent!] many of the Gentiles shall say: A Bible! A Bible! We have got a Bible, and there cannot be any more Bible" (2 Nephi 29:3).

Mormonism teaches that they have a progressive religion and that there will be many other "divine" books (like the *Book of Mormon*), so we are not to attach too much importance to the Bible. In verse 10 of that same chapter in the *Book of Mormon,* the cultists have God saying, "Wherefore, because that ye have a Bible ye need not suppose that it contains all my words, neither need ye suppose that I have not caused more to be written." There you have it! They thus lie for God to try to make us believe that the

Bible is not final and that God also will speak to us through Mormon books and papers at later dates.

Banish the Book!

Anyone who wants to have a successful false religion must first get rid of the Bible. Thus, Christian Science has its *Science and Health With Key to the Scriptures*, Jehovah's (false) Witnesses have their own souped-up "per-version" of Scripture, and Catholics had to come up with their own "version" to step down the voltage on the Word of God. Seventh-day Adventists have their "sacred writings" of Ellen G. White, and on and on.

But no cult has so revered the writings of their patron saint as the Mormons have their devotion to the *Book of Mormon.* In 2 Nephi 26:20, 21 they criticize the "many churches" other than their own. On pages 92–100 they have a mixed-up hodgepodge of Scriptures, taken from the Bible and thrown in with their own ramblings so that none of it makes sense. On page 100 they (in V:29) ridicule those of us who say that we need no more of the Word of God—that the Bible is all we need.

On pages 104 and 105 the *Book of Mormon* teaches water baptism and works for salvation in plain contradiction to the Bible. For instance, in 2 Nephi 31:17 he says, "For the gate by which ye should enter is repentance and baptism by water," and in verse 20, "Wherefore ye must press forward with a steadfastness in Christ, having a perfect brightness of hope, and a love of God and of all men. Wherefore, if ye shall press forward, feasting upon the word of Christ, and endure to the end, behold, thus saith the Father: Ye shall have eternal life!"

Pages 116, 117 and 122, 123 particularly show how Joseph Smith imitates with his own cheap version of the Scriptures.

Samples of the amateur way he tries to write his "holy book" are on page 125, "the wrestle which I had," and on page 132, "for thus it whispereth me."

Some of the strange made-up names are on pages 152,

182, 215, 221, 222, 249, 250 and 305. Names like Zeez-rom, Zarahemla, Zeniff and Zarahemnah. Amulek is another along with Muloki and Middoni. On page 273 he has the Zoramites; and on page 275, a place called Rameumpton.

Nephites and Lamanites

Much of the *Book of Mormon* (that is not stolen Bible) records the alleged battles between the supposed Nephites and Lamanites. Especially is this true in the Book of Alma. Smith uses "and it came to pass" in verse after verse of the *Book of Mormon,* supposedly to make it sound more like the Bible. Also a host of *thous, thees,* and *wherefores.* Much of the book of Matthew from the Bible you will find in 3rd Nephi. Anything that is good or even sensible was stolen from the Bible. Either that, or he takes Scripture and changes it around a bit to sound official, as in Moroni 7, page 512. One of the samples of how weird this twisting can be is found in Moroni 8:25, 26.

In Alma 5:27–31 (page 207) Mormonism teaches that one must be stripped of pride, envy, mocking one's brother, etc., or he cannot be saved. The book is mass confusion, for on page 141 he speaks of salvation through the atonement of the Saviour.

Look at this little gem: "Adam fell that men might be; and men are that they might have joy." This is on pages 54, 55 in 2 Nephi 2.

Many New Testament verses are supposedly quoted in 588 B.C., hundreds of years before they were uttered or written!

I have so many notes before me of errors, conflicts, and contradictions in the *Book of Mormon* that I could easily fill a book just with these, but you have by now read enough to get the picture. God certainly does not deny Himself. He is not the author of confusion, as the Bible states. It is impossible to believe both Mormonism and the Bible! If you want one good reason why Joseph Smith had to die young and a proof that he was a false prophet, read Deuteronomy 18:20–22.

Gordon H. Fraser's excellent book, *What Does the Book of Mormon Teach?* (Moody Press), is an examination of the historical and scientific statements in the *Book of Mormon*. It is a real eye-opener! Dr. Fraser agrees with me that "the *Book of Mormon* is void of any literary content, credible history, biography, romance or ethical teaching," and thus will not be read or analyzed in a thoughtful manner by anyone.

Mormons insist that their book is the inspired Word of God and "the most perfect book that was ever written" in spite of hundreds of corrections since the first edition. Fraser, along with other scholars, writes: "One could proceed through the entire *Book of Mormon* and find some gross blunder in discernment or fact on every page of the book, all of which betrays the fact that the writer was totally uninformed in spiritual matters and unforgivably careless as a researcher and journalist."

On page 46 of his book Fraser explains the problem of the Indians that the Mormons claim used to be Jews. When the scales fell from their eyes, they became "white and delightsome" [in 1981 changed to "pure and delightsome" (2 Nephi 30:6)] which would seem to declare that the dark ones were evil and the light ones were good (p. 46 of Fraser's book).

On page 56 Fraser reveals that the metals the *Book of Mormon* claims the Nephites used were not even in existence here then.

On pages 60 and 61 Fraser shows how the warriors described in the *Book of Mormon* could not possibly have used the weapons and horses they were supposed to have used because such were not available at that time. For instance "swords of steel" were supposedly used, but there was no steel then. The other metals mentioned here were also unknown at that early date. Also there were no horses here. Early Americans had no horses until after the Spanish conquests, historians know.

Again and again the errors show up in this so-called

Book of Mormon. (See Fraser's comments on silk on page 71 and steel on page 75.) Churches and synagogues are proven to be unheard of in those early days before Christ (page 72 in Fraser's book) though Joseph Smith has mentioned both again and again. Dr. Fraser sums it all up by saying on page 90 as he comments on the errors and discrepancies in the *Book of Mormon:*

No such population ever existed in ancient America.

No such civilization ever existed in America.

Silk was introduced by the Spaniards.

Early Americans had no horses or beasts of burden. Ancient Americans had no gold or silver until 1,000 years after this time. Obviously, they had no steel for swords.

Over and over he proves that Mormonism was a fraud if we are to equate it with the *Book of Mormon.*

Fraser concludes: "The *Book of Mormon* teaches confusion, contradiction and chaos. It teaches salvation by self rather than by the Lord Jesus. It refers to script, weapons, coins, textiles, synagogues and temples that never existed."

Where Are Those Plates?

Some other things the Mormons have not explained: Where are the supposed "gold plates" now? What did Smith do with them? If the Mormon church had them, you may be sure they would be in a gorgeous museum which the world, for a price, could see!

Why are Indians now still Indians? If early Jews came over here and became Indians, why do Jews now not so progress? And why do Indians never show any Jewish characteristics?

Why did God use such poor grammar in the *Book of Mormon?* Mormons teach that "every word and every letter was given to Joseph Smith by God," and yet there were so many instances of poor grammar and bad English in the original copies that they have had to be corrected many times over. Even when God spoke through ignorant fishermen disciples like Simon Peter, He used good grammar. As

Mormon leaders became better educated, they were so humiliated by the many errors in the *Book of Mormon* that Floyd McElveen states they made some 4,000 changes in grammar, punctuation and word structure. However, as McElveen reminds us, Joseph Smith's grammar was perfect when he copied verbatim from the King James Bible!

Smith was supposed to have had 3 witnesses who swore that they really saw the "gold plates." Later Martin Harris admitted he only saw them with the "eye of faith." The others said they saw them when they were wrapped up or covered!

The *Book of Mormon* was supposed to have been in "reformed Egyptian." But scholars in the languages say it had to be a hoax, that there was no such thing as reformed Egyptian. McElveen in his book, *Will the Saints Go Marching In?* has an excellent treatment of this on pages 53–56.

With the exception of (Mormon) Brigham Young University, the great institutions all declare, "There is no evidence whatever of any migration from Israel to America, and likewise no evidence that pre-Columbia Indians had any knowledge of Christianity or the Bible" (McElveen, page 64). Anthropologists declare that Indians are not the descendants of Israelites as the Mormons claim. The *Book of Mormon* is a fraud. I wonder, too, if those great cities and temples existed here, why have they never been located? Other ancient cities have.

Joseph Smith's mother wrote that "Joseph as a boy would give the most amusing recitals imaginable as he would describe the ancient inhabitants of the country, their dress, mode of travel, and the animals on which they rode. Their buildings, their cities, their mode of warfare and also their religious worship he would do with as much ease as if he had spent his whole life with them." Yes, Joseph Smith had a vivid imagination, indeed.

Where did the *Book of Mormon* come from? Partly from the vivid imagination of Smith, no doubt, but partly also from a book of that time written by Sidney Rigdon who, according to report, joined forces with Joseph Smith to vent his spleen against Alexander Campbell with whom he had severed relations. (Could this partly explain the similarity of Mormonism with Campbellism on such matters as baptism and salvation by works?)

A Solomon Spaulding had a manuscript that Rigdon made available to Smith. Some believe that Rigdon collaborated with Joseph Smith to concoct the *Book of Mormon.* Rigdon, who had been quite active in the Campbellite movement, understood the religious life and terminology of the day. Rigdon had posed as John the Baptist. Smith and his co-writer Oliver Cowdery were supposed to have taken time off to go to the woods and pray and to have had a "visitation" from John the Baptist! Some believe Smith stole the whole idea from Spaulding's novel.

Whichever of these men had the most to do with fabricating the *Book of Mormon,* we need to remember that Satan is behind all false religion. Men can be used of the Devil and not know it. Revelation 2:2 commends the church of Ephesus who "tried them which say they are apostles, and are not." So we can still expect those in false religious circles who will say they are apostles when, of course, they are not. The Devil comes as "an angel of light" which could well account for the angel Moroni. Maybe Joseph Smith the "glass looker" did see an angel, but it could have been one of Satan's angels (II Cor. 11:14; Matt. 25:41).

The apostle Paul by inspiration of God says, in the Bible, "But though we, or an angel from heaven, preach any other gospel unto you...let him be accursed" (Gal. 1:8).

Holy Underwear and Other Fetishes

"Mormonism is a major cult hiding under the disguise of Christianity," writes Hal Mason; and no one could have stated it better. False religions always have enough truth to float the falsehood, and that's why Mormonism uses the Bible. It doesn't believe the Bible; it *uses* the Bible to promote its heresy.

False religions are fleshly as well as devilish. The flesh always wants something to see, to feel, to cling to, other than the plain Word of God. So the Catholic wants his burning candles, confessional booths, prayer beads, and holy water. The charismatic wants his tongues experience (as some Mormons do), his great and warm feelings of ecstasy, and his rock-beat music to keep him jumping and swaying in rapture. Hare Krishna and other mystical oriental religions want their chanting and trances.

Mormons are no exception. Hal Mason reminds us that fetishism is "the belief in the magical efficacy of various objects, either natural or artificial, when employed as talismans to promote fertility, cure disease, and ward off injury." The Catholic has his idols in the yard or on the dashboard of his car. The voodoo worshiper in Haiti or Africa has his beads, whips, or a ring in his nose. The Mormon has his holy underwear! In this he is no different from other pagans with their medicine bags and voodoo charms.

47

Those who have been through the temple are supposed to wear these garments for the rest of their lives. Mason writes that the old style garments resembled a union suit and most Mormons wear only the old style in the temple. The modern garment is much abbreviated to go with modern clothing.

Mystic signs are embroidered on them to remind the Mormon of his temple obligations. There is a mason's square over his right breast as a reminder of his covenants. There is a compass over his left breast to remind him that his passions and appetites must be kept under control. The navel mark speaks of his constant need of nourishment to body and spirit. There is a knee mark to remind him of his confession of Christ. The holy underwear is to provide protection and blessing and therefore is no different from fetishes worn by primitive pagans who depend upon charms and other objects in a superstitious way.

Mormons also believe in animism or the theory that animals, fish, fowl, and birds were first created as distinct spirits and existed in spirit form before they were created naturally on the earth.

Grabbing at a Stick

Mormons I have talked to immediately start in on the two sticks of Ezekiel 37. They say that one of the sticks is the stick of Joseph Smith (how fortunate that his parents thus named him!). No matter that there were other Josephs in the Bible. The other stick in Ezekiel's prophecy is the stick of Judah. Mormonism teaches that "the stick of Judah" refers to the Bible and "the stick of Joseph" refers to the *Book of Mormon.* The joining of the two sticks is supposed to mean that God brought the *Book of Mormon* together with the Bible as His revelation to man.

Once more the Mormons have dishonestly taken the text from the context to make a pretext. Read the chapter, and we immediately see that God is not talking about books or records but about people and nations! Read the whole "dry bones" portion of the chapter, and it becomes clear. God is using the two sticks to describe the gathering together of the two separated groups of Israelites (Judah 2½ tribes) and Israel (9½ tribes). This prophesies the restoration of Israel in the land of Palestine, not Mormons in Missouri or Utah! Mormons, like most cultists, take an obscure portion of Scripture and try to make it fit into some major doctrine instead of interpreting the obscure in the light of the plain teaching of the Bible. This is how the Campbellites get so carried away with water baptism and the charismatics with their "unknown tongues"!

Harley Johnson writes:

> When we interpret the Bible in its context and take the words of the Bible to mean literally what they say, we find that it would be impossible for Ezekiel 37 to teach that the Bible is the stick of Judah and that the *Book of Mormon* is the stick of Ephraim.
>
> 1. Ezekiel was the one who was to do the writing.
>
> A. The one stick for Judah and for the children of Israel could not be the Bible. The Bible was written on 66 separate scrolls by 40 men over a period of 1600 years, not by Ezekiel in one lifetime.
>
> B. The other stick for Joseph, the stick of Ephraim, could not be the *Book of Mormon* because it was supposed to have been written by Mormon and Moroni as an abridgment of ancient records. Again, Ezekiel was not the author of the abridgment or the ancient records.
>
> 2. Ezekiel knew fully the difference between a "stick" and a "roll of a book."
>
> A. Ezekiel 2:9–10: "And when I looked, behold, an hand was sent unto me; and, lo, a roll of a book was therein; And he spread it before me; and it was written within and without: and there was written therein lamentations, and mourning, and woe."
>
> B. The Hebrew word translated "stick" in Ezekiel 37 is pronounced "ets," and is translated in the Old Testament by ten different English words: 1) gallows, 2) helve, 3) plank, 4) staff, 5) stalk, 6) stick, 7) stock, 8) timber, 9) tree, 10) wood. It is never translated "roll," "scroll," "book," "record," "parchment," "plate," or "papyri."

3. Ezekiel 37:15–17 speaks of one stick for Judah and for the children of Israel his companions and another stick for Joseph, the stick of Ephraim. Even if we were to accept the idea that the sticks referred to by Ezekiel are books, still the *Book of Mormon* could not fulfill this prophecy. In order to fulfill this prophecy, the Nephites (who were supposed to have written the *Book of Mormon*) would have to be descendants of Joseph through his son EPHRAIM (Ezek. 37:16). The *Book of Mormon*, however, teaches otherwise. "And Aminadi was a descendant of Nephi, who was the son of Lehi, who came out of the land of Jerusalem, who was a descendant of MANASSEH, who was the son of Joseph who was sold into Egypt by the hands of his brethren" (Alma 10:3).

4. The *Book of Mormon* was supposed to have been written on plates of gold and plates of brass, not sticks. Never is there any reference in the *Book of Mormon* to that book having been written on "scrolls," "parchment," "papyri," or "sticks."

The Bible does not predict the *Book of Mormon*, nor is there any need for another witness that Jesus is the Christ. There are 66 books in the Holy Bible; and John 20:31 says, "But these are written, that ye might believe that Jesus is the Christ, the Son of God; and that believing ye might have life through his name."

12

Who Is Head of the Church?

God declares in the Bible that Christ is the head of the church (Eph. 1:20–23). In fact, these verses exalt Him as the head of all things, "Far above all principality, and power, and might, and dominion, and every name that is named, not only in this world, but also in that which is to come: And hath put all things under his feet, and gave him to be the head over all things to the church, Which is his body, the fulness of him that filleth all in all."

Satan hates the headship of Christ and has manifested his hatred through Mormonism and Mormon leaders. But "Christ is the head of the church: and he is the saviour of the body" (Eph. 5:23).

Rejecting the truth of the headship of Christ, the Mormons say that God is an exalted man. They teach that Christ and the Devil were brothers, that Christ was married to multiple wives, that the Holy Spirit is but a fluid or substance, that all men are brothers (like modernists teach), that people raise children after they leave this earth, and that Ezra Taft Benson, senior member of the Council of the Twelve Apostles, is the head of the church (or whoever happens to be the president of the Mormons when you read this).

The president of the Council of Twelve rules the Mormon church. They teach the restoration of the Melchizedec and Aaronic priesthoods and then have a president, counselors, presiding bishops and general auxiliary boards, all to keep the corrupt organization going.

Mormonism claims that the Lord sent John the Baptist to Joseph Smith to ordain him to the Aaronic priesthood. They also claim that Peter, James, and John laid their hands on Smith.

But when Christ died on the cross, He fulfilled the types of the Old Testament priesthood and offerings perfectly. The Aaronic priesthood was thus done away with as the book of Hebrews plainly reveals. And only Christ ever held the Melchizedec priesthood.

Mormons try to usurp power that does not belong to any person—Christian or otherwise. But the Christians they condemn are the only people who are truly priests (Rev. 1:6)! We belong to the royal priesthood (I Pet. 2:9), and Christ is our High Priest in the heavens forevermore (Heb. 4:14–16). To try to claim this priesthood for Mormon cultists is the rankest kind of blasphemy.

Dr. Bruce Kinney, late head of a Baptist mission in Utah, well declared: "The whole system [of Mormonism] is based upon a bogus book, rotten revelations, tricky translations, a profligate prophet, a counterfeit creed; it is being propagated today by a profiting president, abetting apostles, bigoted bishops, and plundering priests!" Jesus said, "Beware of false prophets, which come to you in sheep's clothing, but inwardly they are ravening wolves" (Matt. 7:15).

Hal Mason says, "Mormonism is a spiritual disease that is almost 100% terminal in those who contract it. A dedicated worldwide program of inoculation is needed to break the chain of transmission."

13

The Secret of Granite Mountain

Joseph Smith, the founder of Mormonism, said: "The greatest responsibility in this world that God has laid upon us, is to seek after our dead" (*Teachings of the Prophet,* Joseph Smith, p. 356; also see *King Follett Discourse,* p. 24).

Unsaved Corinthian pagans once had a practice of baptizing live people in behalf of dead ones. This is probably what Paul referred to in I Corinthians 15:29 (the only place baptism is ever mentioned in connection with "the dead"), or else it might simply mean those living saints who are baptized to take the place of, or to fill in the ranks where once a live Christian stood. At any rate, it is never mentioned again in Scripture and certainly does not mean what Mormons have tried to make it mean.

In full-page color spreads in *Reader's Digest,* the Mormons have made much of Granite Mountain. They boast that "a billion people live" in their archives in the mountain vaults deep inside Granite Mountain, 20 miles south of Salt Lake City. There a broad entry tunnel with a 14-ton door made of steel leads straight into the heart of the mountain to a grid of six arched vaults.

Each vault holds a thousand or more steel filing cabinets each holding 825 rolls of microfilm. Each roll contains names and records by the thousands. These are names left behind in deeds and marriage licenses, family Bibles, parish registers, probate and cemetery lists. Constantly the Mormons are adding more names from all over the world. They claim this is the richest genealogical resource in the world—the vital records of over one billion people, a precious collection which they term "a unique genealogical treasure." These cultists convince people they can be baptized now so that their deceased loved ones listed in Granite Mountain may "have the baptism that Jesus taught in His Gospel." Those who receive this baptism, they say, have the freedom in the spirit world to accept or reject this baptism which, if they accept, they will be born again.

The Mormon church thus offers vicariously the salvation which God says in the Bible a person must get in this life or be eternally lost. Any false religion which makes sinners feel they can go on in their sins and still have a chance to miss Hell after death is going to be popular with those sinners!

A Mormon leader recently said that they are prepared to perform the necessary genealogical research so that all those now or ever in the spirit world can be vicariously baptized. They claim that the great reformer Martin Luther is now a Mormon because they baptized him into the Mormon church by proxy in 1922, some 376 years after his death! How do you like that? Mormons foolishly believe that this is mission work, that baptizing dead people into the Mormon faith will save their souls!

"The spirit of man," said Joseph Smith, "is not a created being; it existed from eternity and will exist to eternity" (*Teachings of the Prophet,* Joseph Smith, p. 158). So the weird and unscriptural notions of a fortunetelling heretic over 150 years ago has brought about this amazing collection of names in Granite Mountain.

Harley Johnson, missionary to the Mormons, comments on the statement of the "Prophet" Joseph Smith when he says: "The greatest responsibility in this world that God has laid upon us is to seek after our dead."

Johnson well declares:

> It does seem strange, if doing temple work for the dead is the GREATEST RESPONSIBILITY and the

GREATEST COMMANDMENT, that Jesus never mentioned it once.

When Jesus was asked by one of the scribes, "Which is the first commandment of all?" Jesus' answer was, "The first of all the commandments is, Hear, O Israel; The Lord our God is one Lord: And thou shalt love the Lord thy God with all thy heart, and with all thy soul, and with all thy mind, and with all thy strength: this is the FIRST COMMANDMENT. And the second is like, namely this, Thou shalt love thy neighbour as thyself. There is none other COMMANDMENT GREATER than these" (Mark 12:28–31).

In the Bible the practice of baptizing for the dead is mentioned only once; and those who practiced baptism for the dead are counted as HEATHEN by the Apostle Paul. "Else what shall THEY do which are baptized for the dead, if the dead rise not at all? why are THEY then baptized for the dead?" (I Cor. 15:29).

If the Apostle Paul practiced baptism for the dead, or had the Christians at Corinth practiced baptism for the dead, why didn't he say, "Else what shall I do..." or "Else what shall we do..."? Instead, Paul refers to a heathen practice and says, "Else what shall they do...."

Furthermore, even though this writer does not accept the *Book of Mormon* as the Word of God, that volume never once mentions baptism for the dead! The word baptism appears 25 times in the *Book of Mormon*. The word baptize is used 28 times. The word baptizing appears 6 times; and the word baptized, 85 times. However, the doctrine of baptism for the dead IS NOT mentioned even one time!

The Bible teaches: "He that believeth on the Son hath everlasting life: and he that believeth not the Son shall not see life; but the wrath of God abideth on him" (John 3:36).

The *Book of Mormon* teaches: "Ye cannot say, when ye are brought to that awful crisis, that I will repent, that I will return to my God. Nay, ye cannot say this; for that same spirit which doth possess your bodies at the time that ye go out of this life, that same spirit will have power to possess your body in that eternal world. For behold, if ye have procrastinated the day of your

55

repentance even until death, behold, ye have become subjected to the spirit of the devil, and he doth seal you his; therefore, the Spirit of the Lord hath withdrawn from you, and hath no place in you, and the devil hath all power over you; and this is the final state of the wicked" (Alma 34:34–35).

Doctrine and Covenants, section 42, verse 12, states: "And again, the elders, priests and teachers of this church shall teach the principles of my gospel, which are in the Bible and the *Book of Mormon,* in the which is the fulness of the gospel" (Section 20, verses 8, 9).

If the Bible and the *Book of Mormon* contain the fulness of the gospel, as is stated above, and neither of them teaches baptism for the dead, those who teach this practice are teaching a FALSE DOCTRINE!

Celestial Marriage

Further, married couples, they say, who have paid tithes to the Mormon church, kept their church vows and been loyal to the Mormon system, can be married in the Mormon temple and are thus sealed in a celestial marriage that is binding for all eternity. These people will become gods and will go on reproducing even after physical death. This again is totally unscriptural.

Sandra Tanner, in her enlightening book, *The Bible and Mormon Doctrine,* quotes Mormon Milton Hunter, "The crowning gospel ordinance requisite for Godhood is CELESTIAL MARRIAGE." This means temple marriage, and most Mormons strive for this dubious honor.

Mrs. Tanner in the same book quotes from *Mormon Doctrine,* page 238: "The opposite of eternal lives is eternal deaths...those who do not have spirit children eternally are said to inherit the deaths."

Again from the same Mormon book, "Salvation in its true and full meaning is synonymous with exaltation or eternal life and consists in gaining an inheritance in the highest of the three heavens within the celestial kingdom. The full salvation is obtained in and through the continuation of the family unit in eternity, and those who obtain it are gods!"

A Mormon apostle said, "This glorious principle of eternal marriage did not come to the prophet Joseph Smith by reading the Bible (I guess not!) but by the revelations of the Lord to him."

Those who know the Lord, of course, know that such "revelations" came to Smith from his majesty, the Devil! "If they speak not according to [God's] word, it is because there is no light in them" (Isa. 8:20).

14

Why the Mormon Church Could Not Be of God

Many of the doctrines of the Mormon church are not found in the *Book of Mormon.* Neither are they found in the Bible! The *Book of Mormon* is a fairy tale about expeditions, wars among people who never existed, Jews who became Indians, and patched-up, twisted portions of Scripture stolen from the Word of God. The *Book of Mormon* is not a doctrinal book. Their church doctrines have been made by men from Joseph Smith and Brigham Young right down to this present time.

In the Mormon book, *History of the Church,* Joseph Smith said:

"I am the only man that ever has been able to keep a whole church together since the days of Adam. A large majority of the whole have stood by me. Neither Paul, John, Peter, nor Jesus ever did it. I boast that no other man ever did such a work as I" (pp. 408, 409, Vol. 6).

Such humility is touching, I know.

Oddly enough, many of the cardinal doctrines of the Mormons have no basis in their "holy" *Book of Mormon.* Some of these are:

The organization of the Mormon church.

The Mormon priesthood orders.

The doctrine of plurality of gods.

The idea that God is an exalted man.

Men may become gods.

The doctrines of the three degrees of glory, the pre-existence, and the eternal progression plan.

Secret temple worship.

Genealogies.

Baptism for the dead.

Celestial marriage.

No Authority

Actually, then, Mormons have no basis at all for much of what they believe. It is not found in *their* "Bible" or in God's Word. They have been hoodwinked by a cult that has no authority at all!

In the Bible God warns Christians about "endless genealogies" (I Tim. 1:4) and tells us not to give heed to that or to "fables" which minister questions. In Titus 3:9 God plainly tells us to "avoid foolish questions, and genealogies, and contentions, and strivings about the law; for they are unprofitable and vain." What the Bible plainly warns Christians against, the Mormons spend millions of dollars on in their vaults in Granite Mountain!

Mormonism says in *Doctrines of Salvation* that "there will be comparatively few who will partake of this awful misery and eternal darkness" (of Hell). But our Bible says, "Broad is the way, that leadeth to destruction, and many there be which go in thereat" (Matt. 7:13). Whom will you believe?

Bruce McConkie (*Mormon Doctrine,* p. 670) says, "There is no salvation outside the Church of Jesus Christ of Latter-day Saints." Jesus said, "I am the way, the truth, and the life: no man cometh unto the Father, but by me" (John 14:6). And again, "Neither is there salvation in any other: for there is none other name under heaven given among men, whereby we must be saved" (Acts 4:12).

Of course, every false cult believes their way is the only way. Catholics are taught they must be in the Roman church. Campbellites (Church of Christ people) declare theirs is the only true church and their preacher must baptize you into that church or you are lost. Thus do other cultists believe. The only safe way is to accept what God says in His Word.

Mormon Arthur Richardson says, "The Church of Jesus Christ of Latter-day Saints has no call to carry the gospel to the Negro, and it does not do so." Their church is not God's church, then, for Jesus gave the Great Commission to the church to "go ye into all the world, and preach the gospel to every creature" (Mark 16:15). By this time Mormons have planned to have 45,000 missionaries and predict a conversion rate of nearly 500,000 per year. But Negroes would just have to go on to Hell, according to their church teaching.

(NOTE: In 1978, under pressure, the LDS Church had a "revelation" about accepting blacks. Those close to the situation say, though, that it was a corporate decision. They were getting too much bad press by refusing them any longer. But their church doctrine is still the same about it.

The Lord founded the real church. Jesus is the head of it. The organization is quite simple with a pastor (or bishop) and deacons. Why is the LDS church so complex with president, priesthood, general authorities, counselors, First Council of Seventy, presiding bishops, patriarch to the church, stake organizations, ward organizations, etc.? Did you know that the Mormons claim that their priesthood is a perfect system of government that delivers the human family from all the evils that now afflict it? Even the elements are thus controlled, they say. Will you believe them or believe God?

15

Queer Quirks of Mormonism
Try to Explain These:

Peter Cartright was a godly and famous Methodist preacher who lived at the same time as Joseph Smith. Cartright said, "I found him [Smith] to be a very illiterate and impudent desperado in morals but at the same time he had a vast fund of low cunning."

He constantly hounded Cartright for not claiming the gift of tongues, of prophecy, and the miracles. Smith promised Cartright that he would one day raise up a government in the USA that would overturn the present government and would raise up a new religion that would overturn every other form of religion! Evidently, Joseph Smith always had the idea of founding a religion that would overthrow God and the Bible and put Christianity out of business. Mormons are still attempting to do just that.

Joseph Smith told Cartright that he (Smith) would live and prosper while Cartright died in his sins. But Smith was murdered by a lynch mob while Cartright went on to become one of America's great Methodist leaders. Cartright said the Mormons of Joseph Smith's day would steal the stock, plunder and burn houses; and it was believed they murdered some of the finest citizens of that time. Cartright, who said this, was a presiding elder in the Methodist Episcopal church for about 50 years.

In spite of all of the errors, corrections, and questions in and about the *Book of Mormon*, President Benson of the Mormon church recently said, "The *Book of Mormon* must be enthroned in the minds of our people." He said they believe the book clarifies errors made in the Bible when it was translated from Hebrew. How absurd!

A petition has been drawn up by Christians and through the Utah Missions, Inc., presented to the Mormon church. It is a fervent appeal for them to stop calling themselves Christian and identifying themselves as a church. Citing many of the hideous and unscriptural heresies of Mormonism, the petition rightly says that the teaching of Mormonism bears no relationship to historic Christianity. How true!

Mormonism and Masonry

Why is Mormonism so much like the secret order of Masonry? The Mormon temple oaths are almost identical to the oaths of the Masonic lodge (*Temple Mormonism*, by A. J. Montgomery, pp. 18, 20). Jesus said He did nothing in secret. The Bible forbids oaths. In the Mormon temple, they have to know their passwords and grips in order to enter in through the veil, just as they do in Masonry. They are not in print and must be learned by going over them again and again. Joseph Smith was a Mason, and he and his brother Hyrum held high positions in the brotherhood. This is just one more source of error Smith had for his unscriptural religion.

The "Holy" Boat and "Growing Gold"

The barges in which the early settlers were supposed to have come across the ocean were boats with "a hole in the top and the bottom to let the air in" (Ether 2:20 in *Book of Mormon*). If the water happened to come in with the air, they were to "stop up the hole." I'd have hated to start out across the ocean in a boat without an air vent, to begin with; but I know I would not get outside the harbor if there had to be an air hole in the bottom (Ether 2:20)! Such is the intelligence of Mormon "sacred" writings!

Brigham Young believed that gold, silver, and other metals grew just like the hair on his head or the wheat in the field. Young also taught that the sun and the moon were inhabited (*Journal of Discourses*, Vol. 13, p. 271). How accurate do you want your religious leaders to be?

Smith's "Inspired Version"

Not liking what he read in the Bible, Smith revised it and got him up one to suit him, adding what he thought necessary to exalt the Mormon church he was inventing. But the Smith Bible, though he claimed it was "inspired," is hidden away in Mormon bookstores and not promoted like his other works. The additions Smith made are not only absurd, but he has taken the King James Bible and copied it word for word for about 85–90% of his "Bible"!

Harley Johnson writes: "An example of the changes Joseph Smith made in his 'Inspired Version' is found in Matthew 4:1 where Smith's version says, 'Then Jesus was led up of the Spirit, into the wilderness, to be with God.' This may tell us who Joseph Smith's god was!"

Where Are the Converts?

Someone has well asked, "Where are the converts in Mormonism?" In other words, why do you never hear of anyone who has been transformed by it? Where are the drunks made sober by it? And why are there no Mormon missions on skid row? Is it because they have no real message for the sinner? You guessed it! Christ can instantly change people from addicts to converts, from drunks to sober, law-abiding citizens, from raging, profane sinners to dedicated, loving saints. Cults like Mormonism cannot do this.

The *New York Times* story on Mormonism states, "Despite the pervasive presence of the [Mormon] church in Utah, the state's divorce rate is higher than the national average....Utah also has serious problems with drug abuse, child abuse, and teenage pregnancies"—this despite the fact that at the age of 12 males in good standing are eligible for ordination into the priesthood.

A friend who lived in Utah told me that some young

Utah missionaries had become disillusioned because of the hypocrisy and corrupt living they observed in some who claimed to be faithful Mormons, even among the missionaries.

Mormonism is such a farce as a bona fide religion that men like John L. Smith and his *Utah Evangel* can month after month continue to find errors and oddities to write about. He also can happily report revivals and the results Christian missionaries are having in winning deluded Mormons to Christ.

Smith recently quoted a Brigham Young University professor who said, "In order to understand Mormonism, one should realize that its beginnings were rooted in magic and the occult." Coming from a leading Mormon, that is a rare jewel!

That professor also said before a packed house in Utah that Joseph Smith's father believed in the link between religion and witchcraft and brought up his children in these beliefs. Astrology was also believed in and relied on in the Smith family. The professor said early Mormons were "caught up in the occult."

So the Devil was in this thing from the very beginning, even according to their own professors! How enlightening!

One word of clarification: there is a Reorganized Church of Jesus Christ of Latter-day Saints with headquarters not in Utah but in Independence, Missouri. This small group broke with Joseph Smith over polygamy, claiming he did not write this doctrine. They also rejected others of Smith's teachings but are still Mormons in most of their doctrine. Probably most of them, too, are depending on their works and baptism for salvation, and thus need the Lord.

16

Burning Bosom or Bible Truth?

Mormons are told they get "assurance" that what they read or hear from Mormon leaders is true by a "burning in the bosom." Of course, the Devil can produce such a "feeling." Multitudes of lost religious people are depending upon how they "feel" about it.

I am an evangelist; and I constantly find people who are longing for salvation but have only been told that, if they would "pray through" or "get down before God" or learn to speak in tongues or follow some religious ritual, they would be all right. Followers of great church leaders who preach "positive thinking" sermons tell of the wonderful warmth and the good feeling they get when they have their ears tickled in such services. Surely you want more than a "burning bosom"!

I have before me a book entitled *Forty Years in the Mormon Church and Why I Left It* by Bishop R. C. Evans of Toronto. This is a 173-page volume in which this former priest, bishop, and president of the Mormon church declares it to be "the lying wonder of the latter days"! I also have countless tracts from many, many people who were once Mormons but who have been saved out of the monstrous cult. I could write a book just using their testimonies! These are very real people just like you are who once were snared and deceived by Mormonism but have now found light and wonderful deliverance! This is significant.

Mormonism teaches salvation by works. But God says

it is "not of works, lest any man should boast" (Eph. 2:9). God says it is "by grace...through faith" (Eph. 2:8) in the finished work of Christ. The Bible plan of salvation is so wonderfully simple that it seems absolutely astounding to those who have been trapped in a complex cult. But it is true, nevertheless!

You have seen enough in this book to know what Mormonism really is. Their missionaries were so convincing and positive because they were trained to be, they were programmed to work on you until they had you snowed under with "proofs" that Mormonism was of God. But now you know better. You know that God has warned us in the Bible about these "seducing spirits, and doctrines of devils" (I Tim. 4:1). Mormonism is one of the "damnable heresies" spoken of in II Peter 2:1. You now know that the Mormon plan of salvation and the Bible plan of salvation are poles apart. Both cannot be correct.

It is impossible for God to lie, the Bible assures us in Titus 1:2.

Mormonism tells you that salvation is in the Mormon church and system. God's Word says it is in Christ. "He that hath the Son hath life" (I John 5:12).

Mormonism tells you your sins were washed away in baptism. God says it is through the blood of Christ (Rev. 1:5).

Mormonism says you obtain Heaven by a complex system of doing, striving, and belonging. God says it is a free gift (Rom. 6:23).

Mormonism says Christ died for the sin of Adam. God says He died for our sins (I Pet. 3:18).

Mormonism says Joseph Smith and the LDS Church will save you. God says only Jesus saves (Acts 4:12)!

Mormonism teaches Jesus was a mere man who married and had many wives and children. The Bible says He is King of Kings and Lord of Lords (Rev. 19:16), that He came to be our Saviour, never married, of course, and brings many sons to glory only in a spiritual sense when sinners come to God by Him (Heb. 2:10; 5:9; 7:25).

Jesus is the eternal Rock of Ages. It can be said of Mormonism, "Their rock is not as our Rock, even our enemies themselves being judges" (Deut. 32:31).

Renounce all hope in a false religion, and turn to Jesus today for salvation. Trust Him and Him alone. God says, "Believe on the Lord Jesus Christ, and thou shalt be saved" (Acts 16:31).

Jesus said, "Verily, verily, I say unto you, He that heareth my word, and believeth on him that sent me, hath everlasting life, and shall not come into condemnation; but is passed from death unto life" (John 5:24). What more could you ask?

Books and Other Sources From Which I Have Quoted

I am grateful for the help and inspiration of such books as:

MORMONISM, A MAJOR CULT, by Hal Mason, Baptist Mid-Missions, 4205 Chester Ave., Cleveland, OH 44103

WHAT DOES THE BOOK OF MORMON TEACH? by Gordon H. Fraser, Moody Press, Chicago

WILL THE SAINTS GO MARCHING IN? by Floyd McElveen, Regal Books, G/L Publications, Glendale, CA

THIRTY CULTS AND RELIGIONS, Book 4, by William Dillon, Voice of Melody Publishers, 2506 Rhodes, River Grove, IL 60171

THE BIBLE AND MORMON DOCTRINE, Sandra Tanner, Modern Microfilm Co., Box 1884, Salt Lake City, UT 84110

THE SPIRIT OF TRUTH VERSUS THE SPIRIT OF ERROR (tract), Moody Press, Chicago

THE GIST OF THE CULTS, by J. K. Van Baalen, William B. Eerdmans Publishing Co., Grand Rapids, MI

Various tracts, leaflets, and testimonies

THE GOOD NEWS BROADCASTER magazine (June 1986), Box 82808, Lincoln, NE 68501

THE NEW YORK TIMES MAGAZINE, January, 1986

THE UTAH EVANGEL, by John L. Smith, Editor, Box 348, Marlow, OK 73055

Helps sent to me by Missionary Al Price, working with Northwest Baptist Missions, Box 20480, Salt Lake City, UT 84120

Other factual and reliable literature on Mormonism can be ordered from Ira T. Ransom, 317 W. 7th South, Brigham City, UT 84302; or The Utah Lighthouse Ministry, P. 0. Box 1884, Salt Lake City, UT 84110.

For a complete list of available books, write to:
Sword of the Lord Publishers
P. O. Box 1099
Murfreesboro, Tennessee 37133.

(800) 251-4100
(615) 893-6700
FAX (615) 848-6943
www.swordofthelord.com